SCHOLASTIC

GRADE 1

Morning Jumpstarts:
READING

100 Independent Practice Pages to Build Essential Skills

Marcia Miller & Martin Lee

New York • Toronto • London • Auckland • Sydney
Mexico City • New Delhi • Hong Kong • Buenos Aires

Cover design by Michelle H. Kim
Interior design by Sydney Wright
Interior illustrations by Teresa Anderko, Maxie Chambliss, Rusty Fletcher, Mike Gordon, James Graham Hale, Anne Kennedy, Sydney Wright, and Bari Weissman; © 2013 by Scholastic Inc.
Image credits: Cover photo © 101dalmatians/iStockphoto; page 46: (left) © Santia/Shutterstock; (right) © Paul Broadbent/Shutterstock; page 58: © Dan Barnes/iStockphoto; page 86: used by permission of A de F, Ltd., © 1995; page 98: © Judy Picciotto/iStockphoto

ISBN: 978-0-545-46420-8
Copyright © 2013 by Scholastic Inc.
Published by Scholastic Inc. All rights reserved.
Printed in the U.S.A.
First printing, January 2013.
6 7 8 9 10   40   21 20 19 18 17

Contents

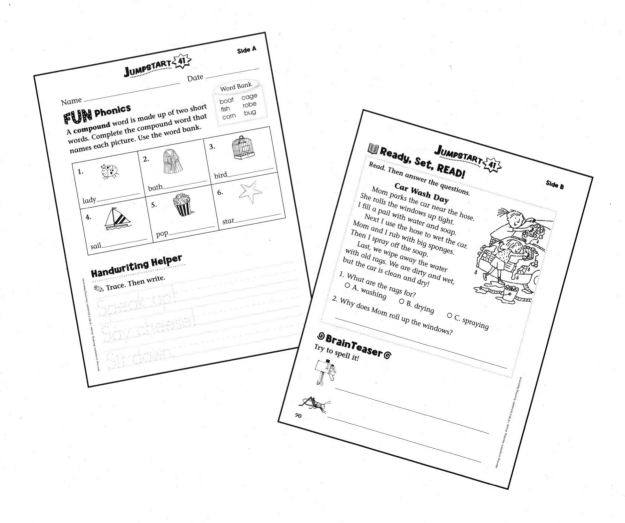

Introduction

In your busy classroom, you know how vital it is to energize children for the tasks of the day. That's why *Morning Jumpstarts: Reading, Grade 1* is the perfect tool for you.

The activities in this book provide brief and focused individual practice on grade-level skills children are expected to master. Each Jumpstart is a two-page collection of four activities designed to review and reinforce a range of reading and writing skills children will build throughout the year. The consistent format helps children work independently and with confidence. Each Jumpstart includes these features:

- Fun Phonics
- Handwriting Helper
- Ready, Set, Read!
- Brainteaser

You can use a Jumpstart in its entirety or, because each feature is self-contained, assign sections at different times of the day or to different groups of learners. The Jumpstart activities will familiarize children with the kinds of challenges they will encounter on standardized tests, and provide a review of skills they need to master. (See page 6 for a close-up look at the features in each Jumpstart.)

The Common Core State Standards (CCSS) for English Language Arts serve as the backbone of the activities in this book. On pages 7–8, you'll find a correlation chart that details how the 50 Jumpstarts dovetail with the widely accepted set of guidelines for preparing children to succeed in reading and language arts.

Generally, we have kept in mind the four CCSS "anchor standards" that should inform solid instruction in reading literary and informational texts, even for the youngest learners. In addition, the activity pages provide children with practice in developing and mastering foundational and language skills, summarized below.

ANCHOR STANDARDS
FOR READING
- Key Ideas and Details
- Craft and Structure
- Integration of Knowledge and Ideas
- Range of Reading and Level of Text Complexity

FOUNDATIONAL SKILLS
- Phonics and Word Recognition
- Fluency

LANGUAGE
- Conventions of Standard English
- Knowledge of Language
- Vocabulary Acquisition and Use

Morning Jumpstarts: Reading, Grade 1 © 2013 Scholastic Teaching Resources

How to Use This Book

Morning Jumpstarts: Reading, Grade 1 can be used in many ways—and not just in the morning! You know the children in your classroom best, so feel free to pick and choose among the activities, and incorporate those you see fit. You can make double-sided copies, or print one side at a time and staple the pages together.

We suggest the following times to present Jumpstarts:

- At the start of the school day, as a way to help students settle into the day's routines.
- Before lunch, as children ready themselves for their midday break.
- After lunch, as a calming transition into the afternoon's plans.
- Toward the end of the day, before children gather their belongings to go home, or as homework.

In general, the Jumpstarts progress in difficulty level and build on skills covered in previous sheets. Preview each one before you assign it, to ensure that the children in your class have the skills needed to complete them. Keep in mind, however, that you may opt for some children to skip sections, as appropriate, or complete them together at a later time as part of a small-group or whole-class lesson.

Undoubtedly, children will complete their Jumpstart activity pages at different rates. We suggest that you set up a "what to do when I'm done" plan to give children who need more time a chance to finish without interruption. For example, you might encourage children to complete another Jumpstart. They might also choose to read silently, practice handwriting, journal, or engage in other kinds of writing.

An answer key begins on page 109. You might want to review answers with the whole class. This approach provides opportunities for discussion, comparison, extension, reinforcement, and correlation to other skills and lessons in your current plans. Your observations can direct the kinds of review or reinforcement you may want to add to your lessons. Alternatively, you may find that having children discuss activity solutions and strategies in small groups is another effective approach.

When you introduce the first Jumpstart, walk through its features with your class to provide an overview before you assign it and to make sure children understand the directions. Help children see that the activities in each section focus on different kinds of skills, and let them know that the same sections will repeat throughout each Jumpstart, always in the same order and position. You might want to work through the first few Jumpstarts as a group until children are comfortable with the routine and ready to work independently.

You know best how to assign the work to the children in your class. You might, for instance, stretch a Jumpstart over two days, assigning Side A on the first day and Side B on the second. Although the activities on different Jumpstarts vary in difficulty and in time needed, we anticipate that once children are familiar with the routine, most will be able to complete both sides of a Jumpstart in anywhere from 10 to 20 minutes.

A Look Inside

Each two-page Jumpstart includes the following skill-building features.

Fun Phonics Every Side A presents a grade-appropriate word-study feature that focuses on a key phonics or word-study topic. For more capable learners, this activity may provide review. Children who need more support may need guidance or hints to help them succeed.

Handwriting Helper This feature rounds out Side A by offering children a chance to practice manuscript handwriting. The words and phrases encompass practice of both lower- and uppercase letters.

Ready, Set, Read! Every Side B begins with a brief reading passage, followed by two or more text-based questions. Passages include fiction and nonfiction, prose and poetry, serious and humorous writing, realistic and fantastical settings. Dig deeper into any passage to inspire discussion, questions, and extension.

Tell children to first read the passage and then answer the questions. Show them how to fill in the circles for multiple-choice questions. For questions that require children to write, encourage them to use another sheet of paper, if needed.

Brainteaser Side B always ends with some form of an entertaining word or language challenge: a puzzle, code, riddle, or other engaging task designed to stretch the mind. While some children may find this section particularly challenging, others will relish teasing out tricky solutions. This feature provides another chance for group work or discussion. It may prove useful to have pairs of children tackle these together. And, when appropriate, invite children to create their own challenges, using ideas sparked by these exercises. Feel free to create your own variations of any brainteasers your class enjoys.

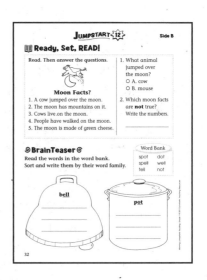

Morning Jumpstarts: Reading, Grade 1 © 2013 Scholastic Teaching Resources

Connections to the Common Core State Standards

As shown in the chart below and on page 8, the activities in this book will help you meet your specific state reading and language arts standards as well as those outlined in the CCSS. These materials address the following standards for students in grade 1. For details on these standards, visit the CCSS Web site: www.corestandards.org/the-standards/.

JS	1.RL.1	1.RL.2	1.RL.3	1.RL.4	1.RL.5	1.RL.6	1.RL.7	1.RL.9	1.RL.10	1.RI.1	1.RI.2	1.RI.3	1.RI.4	1.RI.5	1.RI.6	1.RI.7	1.RI.8	1.RI.9	1.RI.10	1.RF.1	1.RF.2	1.RF.3	1.RF.4	1.L.1	1.L.2	1.L.4	1.L.5	1.L.6
1	•	•	•				•		•											•	•	•	•	•	•	•		•
2										•	•		•		•	•			•	•	•	•	•	•	•	•		•
3										•			•		•	•			•	•	•	•	•	•	•	•		•
4	•	•	•			•	•		•											•	•	•	•	•	•	•		•
5	•	•	•			•	•		•											•	•	•	•	•	•	•		•
6	•	•	•				•		•											•	•	•	•	•	•	•		•
7										•	•	•	•			•			•	•	•	•	•	•	•	•		•
8	•	•	•	•		•	•		•											•	•	•	•	•	•	•	•	•
9	•	•	•			•	•		•											•	•	•	•	•	•	•	•	•
10	•	•		•	•	•			•											•	•	•	•	•	•	•		•
11	•	•	•	•		•			•											•	•	•	•	•	•	•	•	•
12										•	•	•		•		•	•		•	•	•	•	•	•	•	•	•	•
13	•	•	•	•	•	•			•											•	•	•	•	•	•	•	•	•
14										•	•	•	•	•	•	•	•		•	•	•	•	•	•	•	•		•
15	•	•	•			•			•											•	•	•	•	•	•	•		•
16										•	•	•	•	•	•	•			•	•	•	•	•	•	•	•		•
17	•	•	•	•			•	•	•											•	•	•	•	•	•	•		•
18										•	•	•		•					•	•	•	•	•	•	•	•		•
19										•	•	•	•		•				•	•	•	•	•	•	•	•		•
20	•	•	•		•	•	•		•											•	•	•	•	•	•	•	•	•
21										•	•		•			•	•		•	•	•	•	•	•	•	•		•
22	•	•	•		•		•		•											•	•	•	•	•	•	•		•
23										•	•	•		•		•			•	•	•	•	•	•	•	•		•
24	•	•	•		•	•			•											•	•	•	•	•	•	•		•
25										•	•	•	•		•				•	•	•	•	•	•	•	•	•	•

Morning Jumpstarts: Reading, Grade 1 © 2013 Scholastic Teaching Resources

Connections to the Common Core State Standards

JS	Reading: Literature									Reading: Informational Text										Reading: Foundational Skills				Language				
	1.RL.1	1.RL.2	1.RL.3	1.RL.4	1.RL.5	1.RL.6	1.RL.7	1.RL.9	1.RL.10	1.RI.1	1.RI.2	1.RI.3	1.RI.4	1.RI.5	1.RI.6	1.RI.7	1.RI.8	1.RI.9	1.RI.10	1.RF.1	1.RF.2	1.RF.3	1.RF.4	1.L.1	1.L.2	1.L.4	1.L.5	1.L.6
26	●	●	●	●			●	●	●											●	●	●	●	●	●	●	●	●
27										●	●	●	●	●	●	●	●		●	●	●	●	●	●	●	●		●
28	●	●	●	●			●	●	●											●	●	●	●	●	●	●	●	●
29										●	●	●	●			●	●		●	●	●	●	●	●	●	●	●	●
30	●	●	●	●			●	●	●											●	●	●	●	●	●	●	●	●
31										●	●	●	●			●	●		●	●	●	●	●	●	●	●	●	●
32	●	●	●	●			●	●	●											●	●	●	●	●	●	●	●	●
33										●	●	●	●	●		●	●		●	●	●	●	●	●	●	●	●	●
34										●	●		●			●	●		●	●	●	●	●	●	●	●	●	●
35										●	●	●	●	●		●	●		●	●	●	●	●	●	●	●	●	●
36	●	●	●	●	●		●	●	●											●	●	●	●	●	●	●	●	●
37										●	●	●	●			●	●		●	●	●	●	●	●	●	●	●	●
38	●	●	●	●			●	●	●											●	●	●	●	●	●	●	●	●
39										●	●	●	●	●	●	●	●		●	●	●	●	●	●	●	●	●	●
40	●	●	●	●	●	●	●	●	●											●	●	●	●	●	●	●	●	●
41										●	●	●	●		●	●	●		●	●	●	●	●	●	●	●	●	●
42										●	●	●	●	●		●	●		●	●	●	●	●	●	●	●	●	●
43										●	●	●	●		●	●	●		●	●	●	●	●	●	●	●	●	●
44	●	●	●	●	●	●	●	●	●											●	●	●	●	●	●	●	●	●
45										●	●	●	●	●		●	●		●	●	●	●	●	●	●	●	●	●
46	●	●	●	●	●	●	●	●	●											●	●	●	●	●	●	●	●	●
47										●	●	●	●	●	●	●	●		●	●	●	●	●	●	●	●	●	●
48										●	●	●	●			●	●		●	●	●	●	●	●	●	●	●	●
49	●	●	●	●	●		●	●	●											●	●	●	●	●	●	●	●	●
50										●	●					●			●	●	●	●	●	●		●	●	●

Morning Jumpstarts: Reading, Grade 1 © 2013 Scholastic Teaching Resources

Name _____   Date _____

FUN Phonics

Name each picture.
Write the letter for the **beginning** sound.

1. _____ all	2. _____ ey	3. _____ and
4. _____ ig	5. _____ op	6. _____ eb

Handwriting Helper

✎ Trace. Then write.

all

am

and

away

📖 Ready, Set, READ!

Draw lines to match the words and pictures.

Go to the park.

Find a book.

Paint a picture.

Ride a bike.

🌀 BrainTeaser 🌀

Put in order. Write 1, 2, and 3.

Name _____   Date _____

FUN Phonics

Name each picture.
Write the letter for the **beginning** sound.

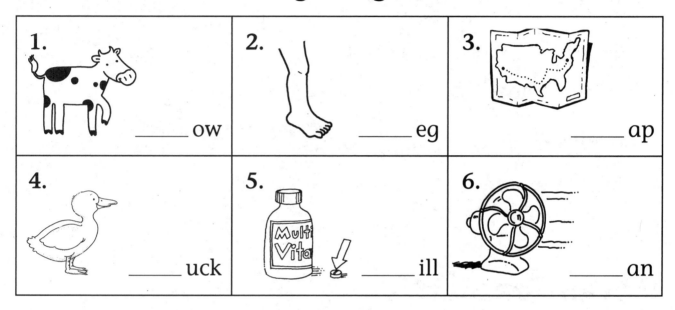

1. _____ ow	2. _____ eg	3. _____ ap
4. _____ uck	5. _____ ill	6. _____ an

Handwriting Helper

✎ Trace. Then write.

but

big

blue

boys

📖 Ready, Set, READ!

Draw lines to match the words and pictures.

In the Sky

Snow falls.

It is raining.

The sun is hot!

It is windy.

Clouds are puffy.

🌀 BrainTeaser 🌀

Connect the dots
in **abc** order.

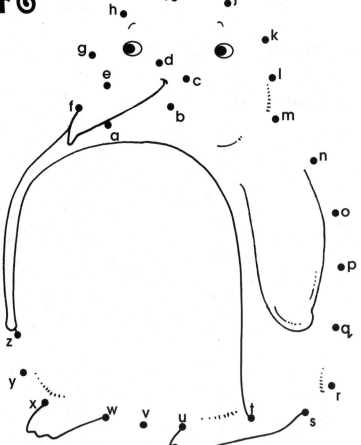

Name _____   Date _____

FUN Phonics

Name each picture.
Write the letter for the **beginning** sound.

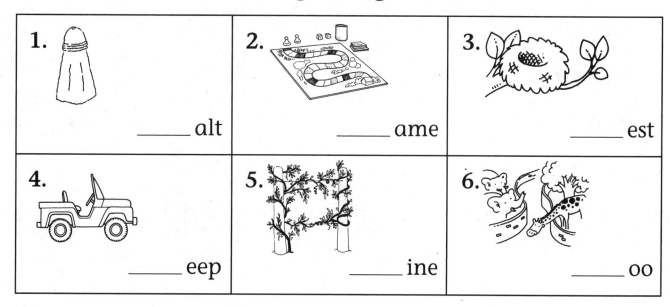

1. _____ alt	2. _____ ame	3. _____ est
4. _____ eep	5. _____ ine	6. _____ oo

Handwriting Helper

✏️ Trace. Then write.

cup

can

come

come

Morning Jumpstarts: Reading, Grade 1 © 2013 Scholastic Teaching Resources

📖 Ready, Set, READ!

Draw lines to match the words and pictures.

At the Zoo

Which animal has . . .

humps?

a tall neck?

stripes?

a big mane?

a long trunk?

🌀 BrainTeaser 🌀

Connect the dots
in **ABC** order.

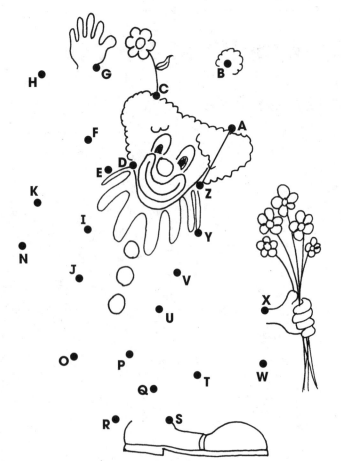

Morning Jumpstarts: Reading, Grade 1 © 2013 Scholastic Teaching Resources

Name _____ Date _____

FUN Phonics

Name each picture.
Write the letter for the **ending** sound.

1. cra _____	2. lea _____	3. boo _____
4. broo _____	5. soa _____	6. bu _____

Handwriting Helper

✎ Trace. Then write.

do

did

dots

down

📖 Ready, Set, READ!

Look at the pictures.

Write Tess or Finn to show who does what.

Tess or Finn?

_____ paints the wall.

_____ draws a car.

_____ mops the floor.

_____ reads a book.

🌀 BrainTeaser 🌀

Draw lines to match letter pairs.

A B C D E F G	H I J K L M
d f g b a c e	k l h j m i

Name _____ Date _____

FUN Phonics

Name each picture.
Write the letter for the **ending** sound.

1. coa _____	2. ja _____	3. fla _____
4. clou _____	5. poo _____	6. moo _____

Handwriting Helper

 Trace. Then write.

find

four

first

funny

📖 Ready, Set, READ!

Read. Then write the names of the frogs in the picture.

Off the Log

Two frogs sit on a log.
"I will hop off," says one.
"I will swim off," says the other.
Hank hops. Suzy swims.
Who is Hank? Who is Suzy?

_____

_____

⊙ BrainTeaser ⊙

Draw lines to match letter pairs.

N	O	P	Q	R	S	T
s	r	p	q	t	n	o

U	V	W	X	Y	Z
x	z	v	u	w	y

Morning Jumpstarts: Reading, Grade 1 © 2013 Scholastic Teaching Resources

Name _____ Date _____

FUN Phonics

Name each picture.
Write the missing letters.

1. _____ a _____	2. _____ e _____	3. _____ i _____
4. _____ o _____	5. _____ u _____	6. _____ u _____

Handwriting Helper

 Trace. Then write.

get

give

glass

going

📖 Ready, Set, READ!

Read. Then answer the questions.

Riddle Time!

What key will never open a lock?

Answer: a tur-key!

What ant can break a table?

Answer: a gi-ant!

1. What **can** a turkey do?
   ○ A. flap   ○ B. draw

2. Giants can break tables because they are

   _____ .

🌀 BrainTeaser 🌀

Color the words.
Use the key.

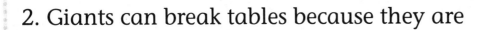

Key

red — Starts With an Uppercase Letter

blue — Starts With a Lowercase Letter

Big	can	You	not	See	kit
old	Dad	tub	Jet	him	May

Morning Jumpstarts: Reading, Grade 1 © 2013 Scholastic Teaching Resources

Name _____   Date _____

FUN Phonics

Name each picture.
Circle the letter that stands for the **middle** sound.

1. h k m	2. g n w	3. c n b
4. d l s	5. n s v	6. n p t

Handwriting Helper

✎ Trace. Then write.

him

her

have

help

Morning Jumpstarts: Reading, Grade 1 © 2013 Scholastic Teaching Resources

📖 Ready, Set, READ!

Read.

Then answer the questions.

How They Go

The bee will fly.
The dog will run.
The pig will walk.
The frog will jump.
The duck will swim.

1. Who will walk?
   - ○ A. the dog
   - ○ B. the pig

2. How does the frog go?

   _____

   _____

🌀 BrainTeaser 🌀

Use the key to color the fish.

Key

1 red	2 pink	3 blue	4 orange
5 brown	6 green	7 purple	8 yellow

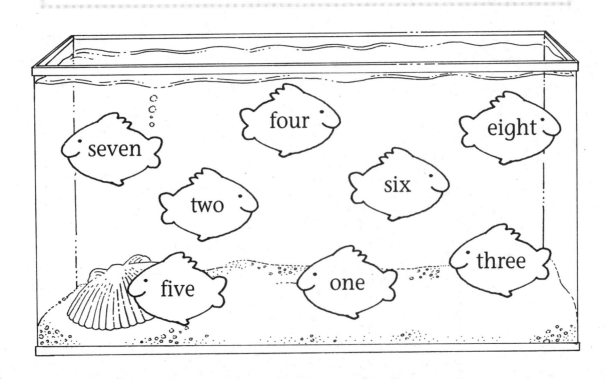

Morning Jumpstarts: Reading, Grade 1 © 2013 Scholastic Teaching Resources

Name _____ Date _____

FUN Phonics

Circle the word that names each picture.

1. 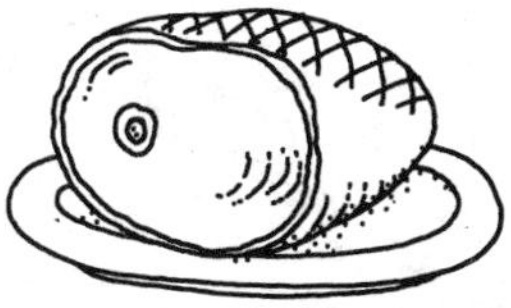 him ham hum	**2.** 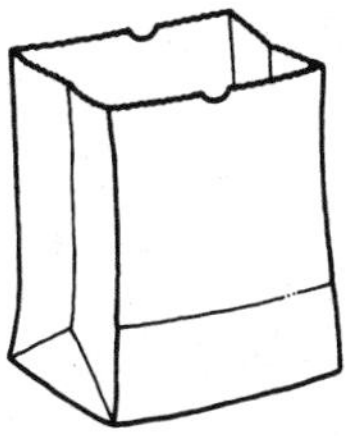 bug big bag	**3.** 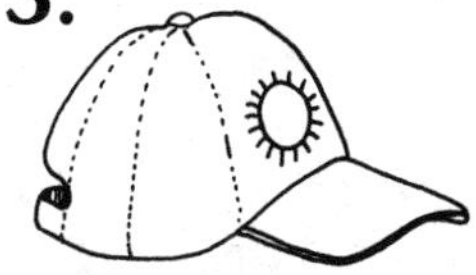 cap cop cup
4.  gas glass grass	**5.**  fun fin fan	**6.**  pad pod bad

Handwriting Helper

✏️ Trace. Then write.

Jet

just

joke

jump

📖 Ready, Set, READ!

Read. Then answer the questions.

What and Why

What is the longest word of all?
Answer: **Smiles**

Why is it so long?
Answer: It has a **mile** between
the first and last letters!

1. What kind of riddle is this?
   ○ A. math riddle   ○ B. word riddle

2. Is **smiles** <u>really</u> a long word? _____

🌀 BrainTeaser 🌀

Read the words in the word bank.
Sort and write them in the chart.

Word Bank		
arm	Gus	hill
hip	Nan	sea

Names	Places	Body Words

Morning Jumpstarts: Reading, Grade 1 © 2013 Scholastic Teaching Resources

Name _____ Date _____

FUN Phonics

Circle the word that names each picture.

1.  cab cob cub	**2.**  crock crook crack	**3.**  lump lamp limp
4.  bend bang band	**5.**  trash train troop	**6.** 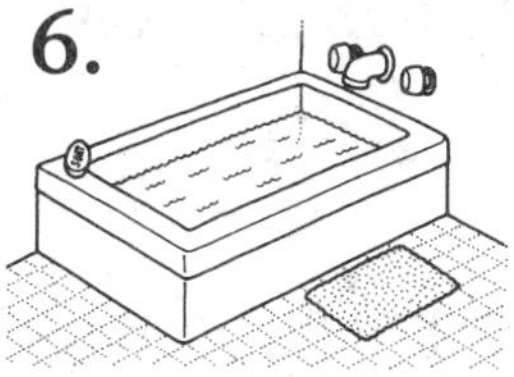 both Beth bath

Handwriting Helper

✎ Trace. Then write.

She

like

books

this

📖 Ready, Set, READ!

Read. Then answer the questions.

Two Jokes

Moo!

Knock, knock!
—Who's there?
Cargo.
—Cargo who?
Car goes **zoom**!

Knock, knock!
—Who's there?
Cows.
—Cows who?
No, silly! Cows **moo**!

1. Both jokes have to do with
   ○ A. doors.   ○ B. sounds.

2. How many questions are in each joke? _____

🌀 BrainTeaser 🌀

Read the words in the word bank.
Sort and write them in the chart.

Word Bank

beef	fig	lamb
grapes	water	milk
plum	tea	ham

Fruits	Meats	Drinks

Morning Jumpstarts: Reading, Grade 1 © 2013 Scholastic Teaching Resources

Name _____   Date _____

FUN Phonics

Circle the word that names each picture.

1.  crab / crib / crop	2.  milk / mike / mush	3.  swing / six / swim
4.  ditch / dash / dish	5.  fast / fist / first	6.  hill / hall / hull

Handwriting Helper

✎ Trace. Then write.

milk

make

much

money

📖 Ready, Set, READ!

Read. Then answer the questions.

Dance Chant

Two hops this way.
Two hops that way.
This way, that way,
this way, that!

Now spin this way.
Now spin that way.
This way, that way,
spin and stop!

1. What do you do last?
   ○ A. hop   ○ B. stop

2. How can the chant help you dance?

   _____

   _____

   _____

   _____

🌀 BrainTeaser 🌀

Read the words in the word bank.
Sort and write them by their word family.

Word Bank

lip	mat
hat	flat
dip	trip

cat

_____

_____

_____

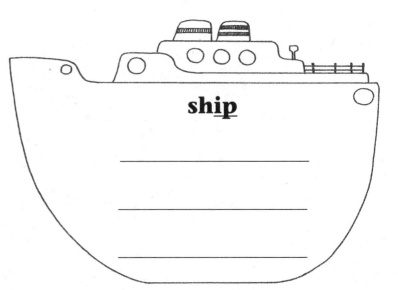

ship

_____

_____

_____

28

Name _____ Date _____

FUN Phonics

Circle the word that names each picture.

1.  lack / lick / lock	2. 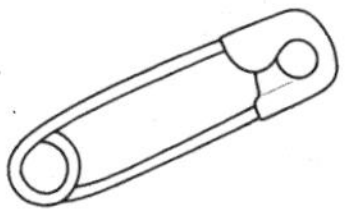 big / bin / pin	3.  king / kiss / kilt
4.  drift / drip / drink	5.  nut / net / knit	6.  clip / clap / click

Handwriting Helper

✎ Trace. Then write.

now

neck

noon

night

📖 Ready, Set, READ!

Read. Then answer the questions.

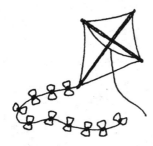

A Wish

Now and then I wish that I could be a kite up in the sky. I'd ride upon the wind and go any way the **breezes** blow.

1. Another word for **breezes** is
   - ○ A. winds.
   - ○ B. storms.

2. What is fun about being a kite?

   _____

   _____

   _____

☉ BrainTeaser ☉

Read the words in the word bank.
Sort and write them by their word family.

Word Bank

tail	twig
wig	Gail
mail	big

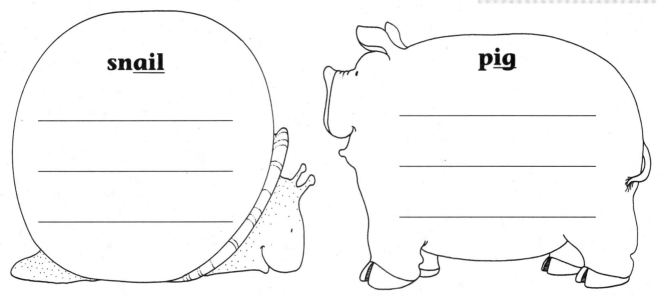

sn<u>ail</u>

_____

_____

_____

p<u>ig</u>

_____

_____

_____

Name _____   Date _____

FUN Phonics

Circle the word that names each picture.

1. 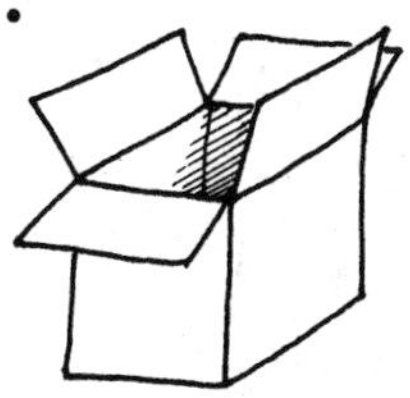 backs bucks box	**2.**  clot cat cot	**3.**  mop mod map
4. 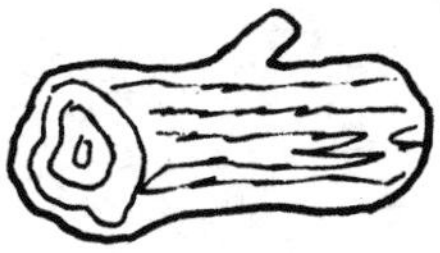 lot let log	**5.**  sack sock sick	**6.**  pond sand pump

Handwriting Helper

✎ Trace. Then write.

one

out

over

older

📖 Ready, Set, READ!

Read. Then answer the questions.

Moon Facts?

1. A cow jumped over the moon.
2. The moon has mountains on it.
3. Cows live on the moon.
4. People have walked on the moon.
5. The moon is made of green cheese.

1. What animal jumped over the moon?
   ○ A. cow
   ○ B. mouse

2. Which moon facts are **not** true? Write the numbers.

   _____

🌀 BrainTeaser 🌀

Read the words in the word bank.
Sort and write them by their word family.

Word Bank

spot	dot
spell	well
tell	not

bell

pot

Morning Jumpstarts: Reading, Grade 1 © 2013 Scholastic Teaching Resources

Name _____   Date _____

FUN Phonics

Circle the word that names each picture.

1. 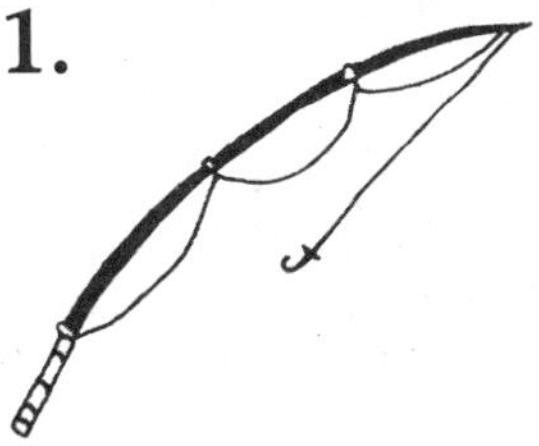 red / rid / rod	2.  stop / slop / shop	3.  lox / figs / fox
4.  fog / frog / from	5.  nab / nub / knob	6.  clock / cluck / click

Handwriting Helper

✎ Trace. Then write.

push

play

picks

Benny

📖 Ready, Set, READ!

Read. Then answer the questions.

So Glad

Rain on the rooftop.
Rain on the tree.
Rain on the grass,
but not on me!

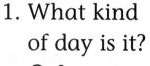

Dry in my raincoat.
Dry in my hat.
Dry in my boots.
Thanks for all that!

1. What kind
   of day is it?
   ○ A. wet
   ○ B. dry

2. Another word
   for **glad** is

   _____.

🌀 BrainTeaser 🌀

Read the words in the word bank.
Sort and write them by their word family.

Word Bank

wink	rock
pink	block
lock	drink

sink

sock

Morning Jumpstarts: Reading, Grade 1 © 2013 Scholastic Teaching Resources

Name _____   Date _____

FUN Phonics

Circle the word that names each picture.

1. 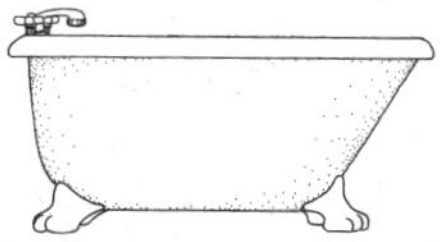 tab tug tub	**2.**  bud bed bad	**3.**  mum mug rug
4.  son sun spun	**5.**  bass boss bus	**6.**  hush hint hump

Handwriting Helper

✏ Trace. Then write.

rain

rest

rope

round

Morning Jumpstarts: Reading, Grade 1 © 2013 Scholastic Teaching Resources

Ready, Set, READ!

Read. Then answer the questions.

Standing Tall

How does a big lighthouse stay up? Here are some facts.

- It is heavy and **sturdy**.
- Its parts fit together well.
- Some of it is under the ground.

1. Which other title best fits the text?
   O A. Made to Last   O B. Not Safe

2. What does **sturdy** mean?

____

BrainTeaser

Write three more words for each word family.

Morning Jumpstarts: Reading, Grade 1 © 2013 Scholastic Teaching Resources

Name _____   Date _____

FUN Phonics

Circle the word that names each picture.

1. 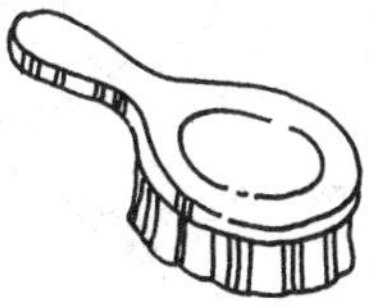	blush brush bush	2. 	dust dish dent	3. 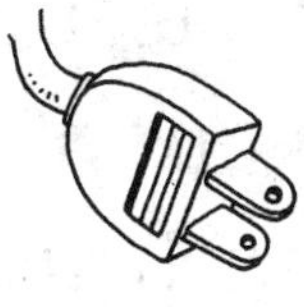	pug pump plug
4. 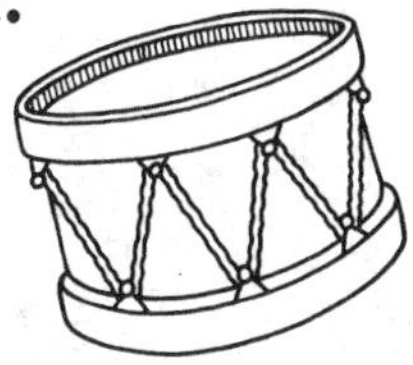	dim dime drum	5. 	track trick truck	6. 	skull skunk sunk

Handwriting Helper

✎ Trace. Then write.

said

slow

spoon

shake

📖 Ready, Set, READ!

Read. Then answer the questions.

Wake Up

Now the night is done.
Time to greet the sun.
Wake up, sleepyhead!
Jump up out of bed.
Make your bed look **neat**.
Have some eggs to eat.

1. When does the poem take place?
   ○ A. night   ○ B. morning

2. What does **neat** mean?

_____

🌀 BrainTeaser 🌀

Write three more words for each word family.

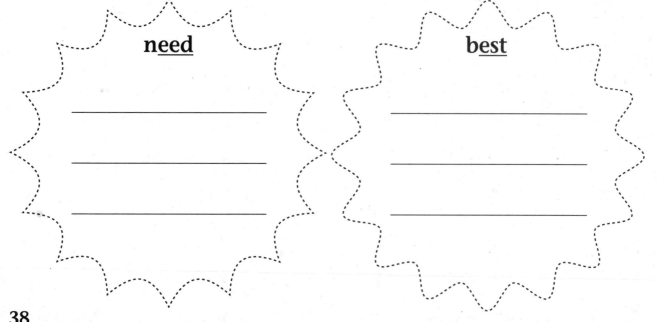

n**eed**

b**est**

Name _____   Date _____

FUN Phonics

Circle the word that names each picture.

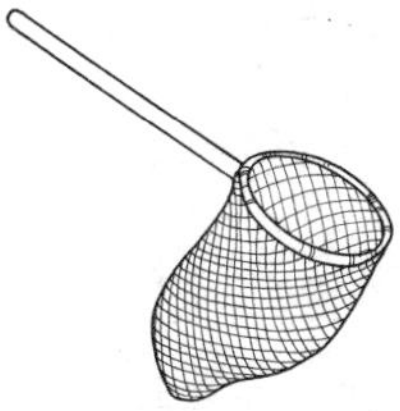

1.	hang	2.	nut	3.	ten
	hunt		net		tint
	hen		knit		tent

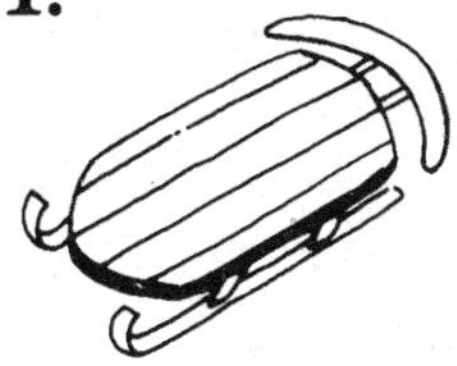

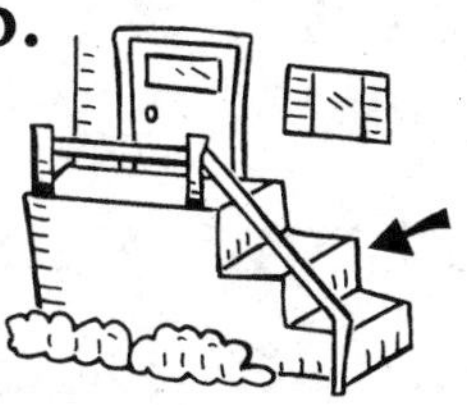

4.	sled	5.	vast	6.	stop
	slid		vest		slap
	slop		vent		step

Handwriting Helper

✎ Trace. Then write.

two

truck

thing

three

📖 Ready, Set, READ!

Read. Then answer the questions.

Your Brain

The brain is a part of your body. It is inside your head. It is safe there.

The brain runs your body. It is like your very own control center. It lets you see, hear, smell, taste, and feel. It lets you talk, think, and dream. The brain is the boss!

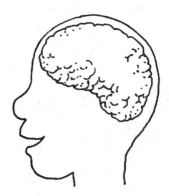

1. The brain is so important because it
   ○ A. runs your body.   ○ B. is on the top.

2. Why do you think your head is hard?

_____

⊙ BrainTeaser ⊙

Fill in the missing word.
Each answer rhymes.

1. sack for old cloths   **rag** _____

2. skinny fish part   **thin** _____

3. baby bird with the flu   _____ **chick**

Morning Jumpstarts: Reading, Grade 1 © 2013 Scholastic Teaching Resources

Name _____   Date _____

FUN Phonics

Circle the word that names each picture.

1.	bolt	2.	shall	3.	check
	built		shell		cheek
	belt		shale		chick
4.	bunch	5.	disk	6.	bend
	band		desk		break
	bench		dusk		bread

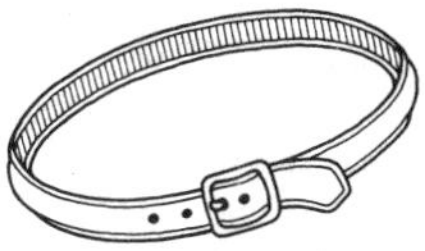

Handwriting Helper

✏ Trace. Then write.

untie

uncle

under

until

📖 Ready, Set, READ!

Read. Then answer the questions.

Let's Bake

Jen bakes cakes.
She bakes white cakes and pink cakes.
Tim bakes pies.
He bakes apple pies and lemon pies.
Sue bakes bread.
She bakes corn bread and white bread.
Which ones do you like to eat?

1. Finish the sentence.
Tim bakes
   - ○ A. bread   ○ B. pies

2. Who bakes cakes?
   - ○ A. Jen   ○ B. Sue

🌀 BrainTeaser 🌀

Write two more words whose letters fit this shape.

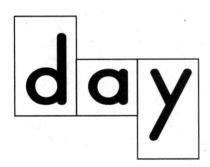
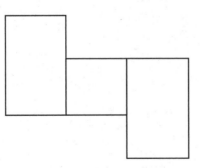
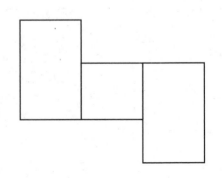

Morning Jumpstarts: Reading, Grade 1 © 2013 Scholastic Teaching Resources

Name _____   Date _____

FUN Phonics

Circle the word that names each picture.

1.  rock / rook / rake	2. 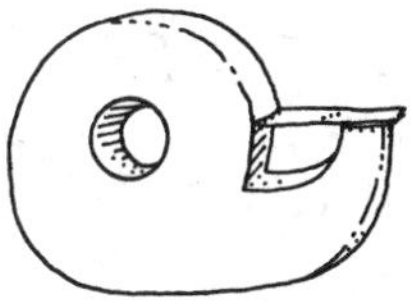 tap / tape / type	3.  vase / vise / ways
4.  wave / whale / wail	5. 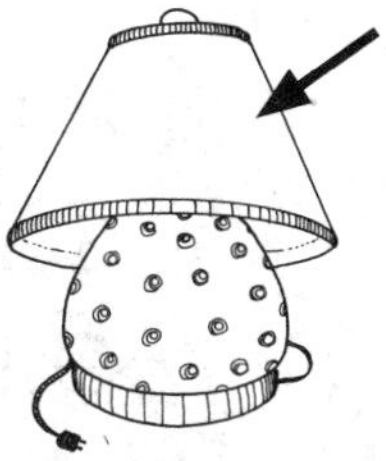 spade / shave / shade	6.  skate / scoot / skit

Handwriting Helper

✏ Trace. Then write.

want

walk

west

where

📖 Ready, Set, READ!

Read. Then answer the questions.

Where Is . . .

Where is my hair?	On my head!
Where is my neck?	Under my head!
Where are my teeth?	In my mouth!
Where are my toes?	On my feet!
Where is my skin?	All over me!

1. What is in your mouth?
   - ○ A. hair
   - ○ B. teeth

2. Which is near your neck?
   - ○ A. your shoulders
   - ○ B. your elbows

⊚ BrainTeaser ⊚

Write two more words whose letters fit this shape.

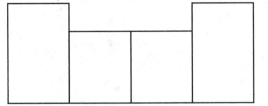

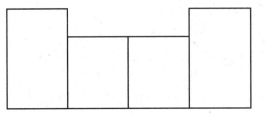

Morning Jumpstarts: Reading, Grade 1 © 2013 Scholastic Teaching Resources

Name _____ Date _____

FUN Phonics

Circle the word that names each picture.

1.	sell sill sail	2.	plain plate place	3.	snail stale sail
4.	try tray tree	5.	pint paint paid	6.	tune treat train

Handwriting Helper

 Trace. Then write.

Andy

Bart

Clay

David

📖 Ready, Set, READ!

Read. Then answer the questions.

Moles, Voles, or Both?

Moles AND Voles
Both have fur.
Both dig a lot.
Both hurt gardens.

ONLY Moles
eat insects.
have big paws.
have long noses.

ONLY Voles
eat plants.
have small paws.
have short noses.

1. What can both animals hurt? _____

2. Which animals eat plants? _____

3. Which animals have big paws? _____

🌀 BrainTeaser 🌀

Write one vowel to spell **two** words.

	t	
l		g
	p	

	b	
w		n
	t	

	m	
c		p
	g	

Morning Jumpstarts: Reading, Grade 1 © 2013 Scholastic Teaching Resources

Name _____ Date _____

FUN Phonics

Circle the word that names each picture.

1. 	noon neat nine	2. 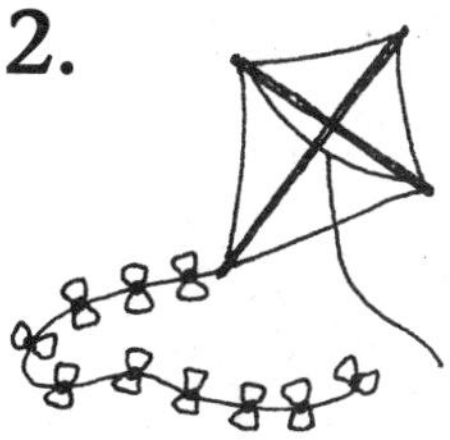	kit kite cut	3. 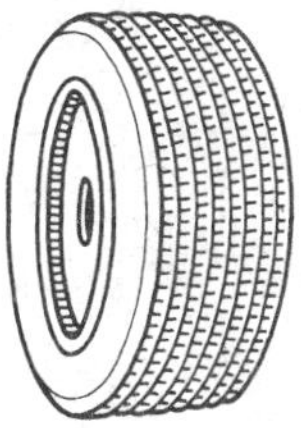	tire tear tore
4. 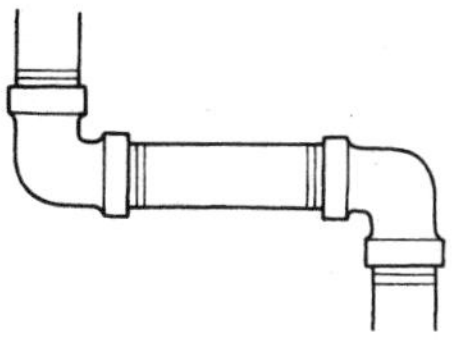	peep pipe pool	5. 	hook heck hike	6. 	dime dice dome

Handwriting Helper

✎ Trace. Then write.

Emma

Flora

Owen

Mattie

📖 Ready, Set, READ!

Read. Then answer the questions.

Fact or Fiction?

Max the cat took a boat ride on the sea. A big wave tipped the boat over. Max fell out. He could not swim.

He was scared. A mermaid saved Max. She took Max to her sea cave. She showed Max her pet starfish.

1. Max could not
   - ○ A. swim.
   - ○ B. ride

2. Who saved Max?
   - ○ A. a boat
   - ○ B. a mermaid

2. What tells you that the story is NOT true?

_____

🌀 BrainTeaser 🌀

What does each sign mean?
Draw lines to match the signs and words.

Trains cross here.   No dogs.   Don't go.

Morning Jumpstarts: Reading, Grade 1 © 2013 Scholastic Teaching Resources

Name _____　　Date _____

FUN Phonics

Circle the word that names each picture.

1.  vine / have / hive	2.  slid / slide / sleet	3.  knife / cuff / fine
4.  mash / mine / mice	5.  smile / smell / small	6.  flee / fly / fry

Handwriting Helper

✎ Trace. Then write.

Inez

James

Kent

Lynn

📖 Ready, Set, READ!

Read. Then answer the questions.

Can It Jump?

Ask an egg to jump. It cannot.
Pick up an egg and put it down.
That is not a jump.
Roll the egg. It can roll.
But that is still not a jump.
AHA! An egg has no legs.
So an egg cannot jump.

1. Why can't an egg jump?

_____

2. AHA! means
   O A. Oh, no!   O B. Oh, I know!

🌀 BrainTeaser 🌀
Read and draw.

- a fish in the water
- a bird by the cloud
- a smile on the sun

Morning Jumpstarts: Reading, Grade 1 © 2013 Scholastic Teaching Resources

Name _____   Date _____

FUN Phonics

Circle the word that names each picture.

1.  come / cane / cone	**2.** 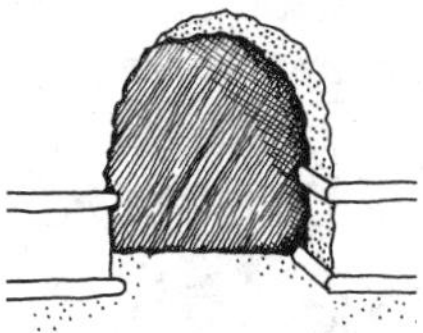 hope / hole / heel	**3.** 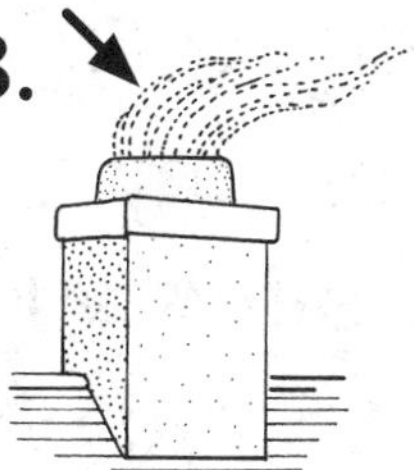 soak / smock / smoke
4. 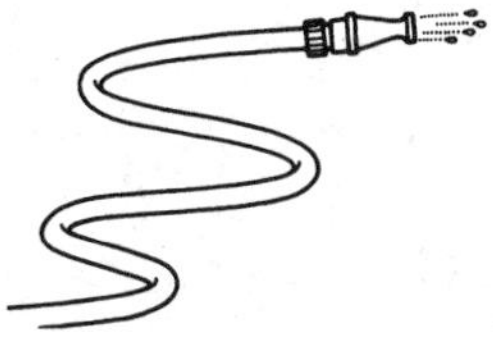 home / hose / house	**5.**  crow / cold / crown	**6.**  food / feed / fold

Handwriting Helper

✎ Trace. Then write.

Maria

Nell

Omar

Peter

📖 Ready, Set, READ!

Read. Then answer the questions.

The Band

"Let us make a band," says Bill.

"I can play drums," says Nan. Boom!

"I can play guitar," says Tom. Strum!

Inez plays a keyboard. She presses the white and black keys. Plink, plunk!

Bill hits a cowbell. Clang! "Now let us rock!" he says. And they all play.

1. Tom can play the

   ○ A. drums.   ○ B. guitar.   ○ C. keyboard.

2. How many kids play in the band? _____

꩜ BrainTeaser ꩜

Finish the man.

- Draw two eyes.
- Draw a ▲ nose.
- Draw a smile.
- Draw a beard.

Morning Jumpstarts: Reading, Grade 1 © 2013 Scholastic Teaching Resources

Name _____   Date _____

FUN Phonics

Circle the word that names each picture.

1. Steve / stove / stiff	**2.** globe / gloom / good	**3.** bow / bowl / blow
4. code / coot / coat	**5.** told / toad / tow	**6.** toast / test / toes

Handwriting Helper

✎ Trace. Then write.

Quinn _____

Rusty _____

Skye _____

Tate _____

📖 Ready, Set, READ!

Read. Then answer the questions.

To Nell's House

1. Start at our school. Turn right onto Lark Way.

2. After three stop signs, turn left onto Bell Road. Drive about two miles.

3. After the car wash, turn right onto Gray Lane. Look for 53 Gray Lane. It is a red house on the left.

1. This is a set of
   ○ A. keys
   ○ B. directions

2. Where does Nell live?

_____

_____

_____

_____

🌀 BrainTeaser 🌀

Look at the pictures.
Find and circle the names for each in the puzzle.
Look across and down.

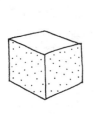

J	T	C	A	G	E	L	R
O	I	U	Q	U	A	K	O
S	R	B	N	E	S	T	S
J	E	E	P	M	R	O	E

Morning Jumpstarts: Reading, Grade 1 © 2013 Scholastic Teaching Resources

Name _____   Date _____

FUN Phonics

Circle the word that names each picture.

1.  moo mile mule	2.  flute fruit fret	3. 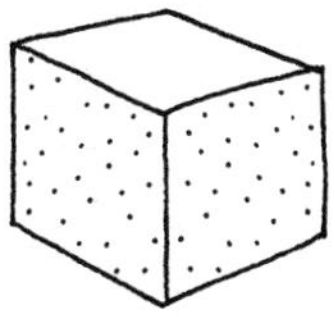 cube code cute
4. 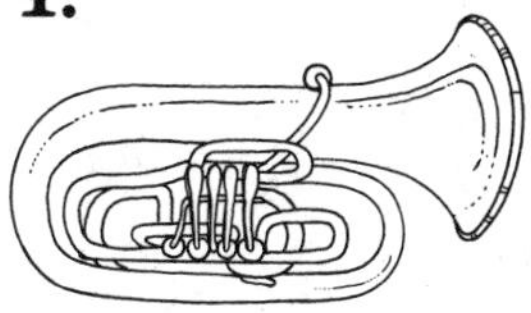 tube tuba tuna	5. 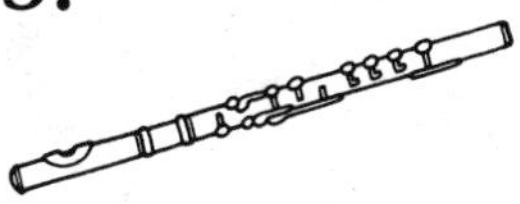 flood fleet flute	6. 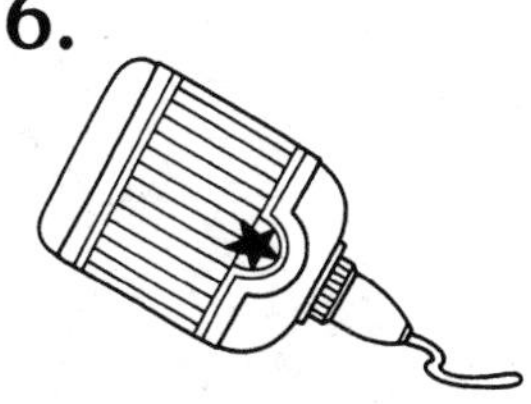 glue goo glee

Handwriting Helper

✎ Trace. Then write.

Una

Val

Winn

Xavier

📖 Ready, Set, READ!

Read. Then answer the questions.

The New House

Today Glen saw his new house. It is not done yet. But he will move soon.

Glen saw his new room. It is big and sunny. It will have bunk beds. Glen hopes he gets to sleep on top.

Maybe moving will not be so bad.

1. What happened today?

   _____

   _____

   _____

   _____

2. How does Glen feel about moving?
   - ○ A. excited
   - ○ B. not sure

🌀 BrainTeaser 🌀

Look at the pictures.
Find and circle the names for each in the puzzle.
Look across and down.

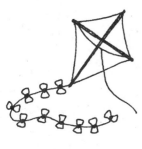

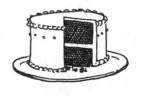

R	O	P	E	K	I	T	H
U	P	A	C	A	K	E	O
B	U	I	S	W	A	N	W
L	A	L	T	K	I	T	E

Morning Jumpstarts: Reading, Grade 1 © 2013 Scholastic Teaching Resources

Name _____   Date _____

FUN Phonics

Circle the word that names each picture.

1. noon new knew	2. duke dune due	3. ruler rail reel
4. soot suit sweet	5. score scare screw	6. juice goose jewels

Handwriting Helper

✎ Trace. Then write.

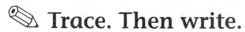

Yoko

Zeke

What name do you like best?

_____

_____

📖 Ready, Set, READ!

Read. Then answer the questions.

Ships

A ship is a large boat.
It can sail a long way.
It can cross wide oceans.
It can go on deep rivers.
    A **cargo** ship can carry giant loads.
A cargo ship can carry oil or pipes.
It can carry steel or cars.
Many things we use get here by ship.

1. What does **cargo** mean?
   ○ A. a large boat   ○ B. a giant load

2. Why don't cargo ships sail on ponds?

_____

🌀 BrainTeaser 🌀

Draw a line to match.

One	More Than One
bat •	• rings
hug •	• plates
ring •	• looks
look •	• hugs
plate •	• bats

Morning Jumpstarts: Reading, Grade 1 © 2013 Scholastic Teaching Resources

Name _____ Date _____

FUN Phonics

Circle the word that names each picture.

1. 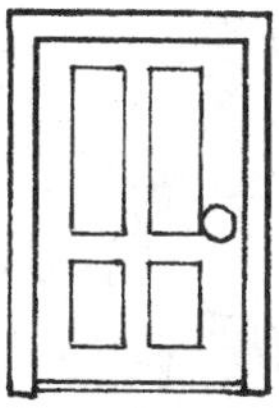 door deer dare	**2.**  shape sharp sheep	**3.**  seed said sand
4.  keen seen queen	**5.**  foot feet felt	**6.** 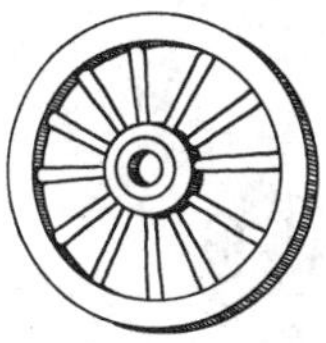 wheel where week

Handwriting Helper

✎ Trace. Then write.

red

pink

green

yellow

📖 Ready, Set, READ!

Read. Then answer the questions.

A Noise

Li and Aya were walking home. They passed a tall tree.

The girls heard a spooky noise. Was it crying? They stopped walking. They held hands.

Then Aya smiled and pointed up. "Look!" she said.

Li saw the kitten. "Oh, kitty!" said Li. "We will get help for you."

1. Why did the girls hold hands?
   ○ A. to cross a street   ○ B. to feel safer

2. What made the noise?

_____

🌀 BrainTeaser 🌀

Finish the chart.

One	More Than One
house	houses
	rooms
	floors
	steps

Name _____   Date _____

FUN Phonics

Circle the word that names each picture.

1. [teacup] tie toe tea	2. [seal] seal sell sill	3. [beans] bone bean bun
4. [leash] leach leaks leash	5. [bird] bleak beak beat	6. [beads] beds beads bends

Handwriting Helper

✎ Trace. Then write.

black

brown

purple

orange

📖 Ready, Set, READ!

Read. Then answer the questions.

Dear Hope,

    It is great at Gem Beach. The ocean is so big! I swim every day. I pick up shells. I make sand castles. It is fun!

    Today I saw a bird dive for food. It flew down fast. Then it came up with a fish in its mouth.

    I miss you. See you soon.

Your Friend,
Dawn

1. Who wrote the postcard?
   O A. Hope   O B. Gem   O C. Dawn

2. Why did the bird dive?

_____

ꙮ BrainTeaser ꙮ

Finish each sentence.

1. Five peaches, but one _____ .

2. Two foxes, but one _____ .

3. Six kisses, but one _____ .

4. Four bushes, but one _____ .

Morning Jumpstarts: Reading, Grade 1 © 2013 Scholastic Teaching Resources

Name _____   Date _____

FUN Phonics

Write a rhyme for each word.
Use an *r* blend from the box.
Use each blend ONCE.

r Blends

br   cr   dr
fr   pr

seen	name	saw
green		

nice	back	loom

Handwriting Helper

✎ Trace. Then write.

now

later

after

before

📖 Ready, Set, READ!

Read. Then answer the questions.

Hungry

Ken rubs his tummy. He is hungry.
So he goes to the diner.
　"A hot dog, please," Ken says.
　"How do you like it?" asks the cook.
　"I like it just plain," says Ken.
　The cook makes Ken's hot dog.
Ken pays her. He eats his hot dog.
He rubs his tummy again. Now Ken is full.

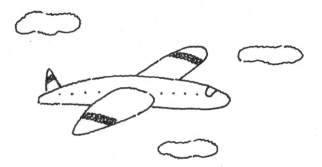

1. Where did Ken go?
　○ A. kitchen　　○ B. diner　　○ C. store

2. What do you like on your hot dog?

_____

🌀 BrainTeaser 🌀

Circle the **action** word.

1. A girl sleeps in her bed.

2. A jet flies in the sky.

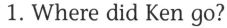

Write an **action** word.

3. A snake _____ in the sand.

4. Jay _____ at the joke.

Name _____ Date _____

FUN Phonics

Write a rhyme for each word.
Use an *l* blend from the box.
Use each blend ONCE.

l Blends

bl fl gl
pl sl

mean	cane	deep
clean		

fast	robe	tag

Handwriting Helper

✎ Trace. Then write.

boy

girl

man

woman

📖 Ready, Set, READ!

Read. Then answer the questions.

Water

You need water every day to live. You get water in many foods you eat.

Apples and carrots have water in them. Milk is part water. Watermelon is full of water. The name tells you so.

Soup has lots of water in it. Ice is water, too. It melts when you suck it.

1. Why does it help to know foods that have water in them?

_____

2. Which food has more water in it?
   ○ A. peach   ○ B. cornflakes

🌀 BrainTeaser 🌀

Write each set of three words in ABC order.

shoe	jump	rib	much	flat	when

Morning Jumpstarts: Reading, Grade 1 © 2013 Scholastic Teaching Resources

Name _____   Date _____

FUN Phonics

Write a rhyme for each word.
Use an *s* blend from the box.
Use each blend ONCE.

> *s* Blends
>
> sc   sm   sn
> sp   st

dirt	rug	dream
skirt		

lace	tile	toot

Handwriting Helper

✎ Trace. Then write.

sister

brother

father

mother

📖 Ready, Set, READ!

Read. Then answer the questions.

Jobs

Bea is a farmer. She works all day. She grows beans. She works hard.

John is a painter. He works every day. He paints pictures. He loves colors.

Lulu is a cook. She works on weekends. She cooks soups. She loves food.

Ron is a dancer. He works at night. Ron teaches people to dance. He loves to dance.

1. Who works at night?
   ○ A. Lulu   ○ B. John   ○ C. Ron

2. Why do you think Lulu is a cook?

_____

☉ BrainTeaser ☉

Write each set of three words in ABC order.

run	start	line	horse	ride	boot

Name _____ Date _____

FUN Phonics

Circle the word that names each picture. Write its <u>final</u> <u>blend</u>.

1.  hard hand hold _nd_	**2.** $2 + 2 = 4$ fact fast find ___	**3.**  chill chest child ___
4.  mark mass mask ___	**5.** 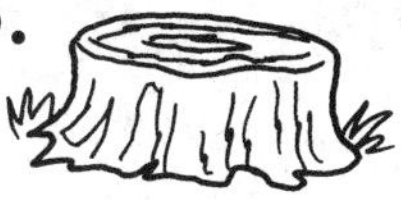 stand stump stamp ___	**6.** 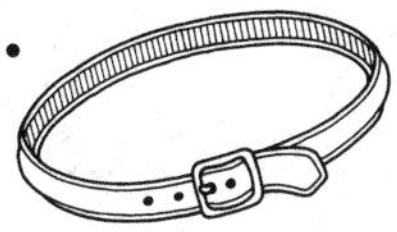 belt best bent ___

Handwriting Helper

✏️ Trace. Then write.

class

desks

chairs

teacher

📖 Ready, Set, READ!

Read. Then answer the questions.

Blue Food

Blueberries are small and round. They grow on a bush. One blueberry bush can grow many, many berries.

At first, blueberries are green and hard. Do not eat them yet. They need time to get bigger. Sun and rain will help them turn blue. Then they are **ripe** and ready to eat. Yum!

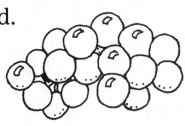

1. Which means the same as **ripe**?
   ○ A. all grown   ○ B. hard   ○ C. round

2. Why do blueberries need sun and rain?

   _____

🌀 BrainTeaser 🌀

Write 1, 2, and 3 to show ABC order.

_____ salt	_____ pipe	_____ ox
_____ rice	_____ bug	_____ post
_____ moth	_____ worm	_____ both
_____ jump	_____ dance	_____ vote

Morning Jumpstarts: Reading, Grade 1 © 2013 Scholastic Teaching Resources

Name _____   Date _____

FUN Phonics

Circle the word that names each picture. Write its <u>final</u> <u>blend</u>.

1.  wasp / want / walk __sp__	2.  best / bird / bend _____	3.  fort / ford / fork _____
4.  stink / stunk / skunk _____	5.  fact / first / fist _____	6.  pound / paint / pest _____

Handwriting Helper

✏ Trace. Then write.

read

write

snail

think

Ready, Set, READ!

Read. Then answer the questions.

Swim Class

Peg did not know how to swim. She asked to go to a swim class. Her mom liked the idea. Peg starts today.

Peg gets to the pool on time. The class has ten kids and two teachers. One teacher helps Peg. Peg learns how to move her arms and legs. Peg and the teacher swim side by side.

1. Why did Peg want to go to swim class?

_____

_____

_____

_____

2. Peg had her class at a
   ○ A. lake
   ○ B. pool
   ○ C. beach

☺ BrainTeaser ☺

Use the picture clues to solve the puzzle.

ACROSS

DOWN

1.

3.

4.

5.

1.

2.

3.

Name _____ Date _____

FUN Phonics

Write the missing digraph
for each word in the sentence.

Digraphs

ch sh th

1. Mom is _____irty years old.

2. I like your new _____irt.

3. Do you like fried _____icken?

4. Please _____ut the door behind you.

5. Use an ax to _____op wood.

6. Can you _____ink of a joke?

Handwriting Helper

✎ Trace. Then write.

ice

river

water

creek

📖 Ready, Set, READ!

Read. Then answer the questions.

Arthur

Do you know the <u>Arthur</u> books? There are lots of them. But once, only two people knew Arthur.

Marc Brown made up Arthur. Mr. Brown was putting his son to bed. The boy asked for a story. Mr. Brown made up an animal named Arthur.

Marc Brown wrote his story as a book. The title was <u>Arthur's Nose</u>.

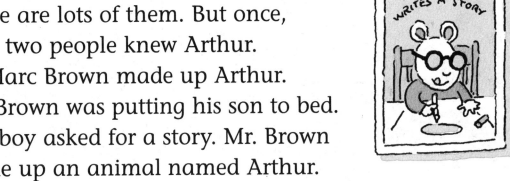

1. Another word for **title** is
   ○ A. author.   ○ B. book.   ○ C. name.

2. Who were the first people to know Arthur?

_____

🌀 BrainTeaser 🌀

Write **a**, **e**, **i**, **o**, or **u** to spell each animal name.

1. f ____ x

2. ____ nt

3. fr ____ g

4. h ____ n

5. d ____ ck

6. p ____ g

Morning Jumpstarts: Reading, Grade 1 © 2013 Scholastic Teaching Resources

Name _____　　Date _____

FUN Phonics

Write the missing digraph
for each word in the sentence.

ph　th　wh

1. My bike has two _____ eels.

2. Dad talks on his cell _____ one.

3. _____ en is it time for lunch?

4. Your ball is over _____ ere.

5. Please take a _____ oto of me!

6. I like _____ is book a lot.

Handwriting Helper

✎ Trace. Then write.

pleased

big smile

so happy

very glad

📖 Ready, Set, READ!

Read. Then answer the questions.

Beads

Kim will make a necklace.
She has red, white, and blue beads.
She needs a loop of string.
It must fit over her head.

Kim cuts white string.
Then she slips beads onto it.
She makes a pattern.

Kim stops when the string
is nearly full. She ties up the ends.
All done!

1. Kim will wear her beads around her
   ○ A. waist   ○ B. wrist   ○ C. neck

2. What colors does Kim use?

_____

🌀 BrainTeaser 🌀

Write **a**, **e**, **i**, **o**, or **u** to spell each color.

1. bl _____ ck   4. bl _____ e

2. br _____ wn   5. y _____ ll _____ w

3. gr _____ _____ n   6. p _____ nk

Morning Jumpstarts: Reading, Grade 1 © 2013 Scholastic Teaching Resources

Name _____ Date _____

FUN Phonics

Write the name for each picture. Listen for the **ng** sound.

1.	2.	3.
_____	_____	_____
4.	5.	6.
_____	_____	_____

Handwriting Helper

✏️ Trace. Then write.

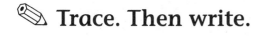

unhappy

all alone

felt blue

sad to say

📖 Ready, Set, READ!

Read. Then answer the questions.

Not Like Its Name

A jellyfish is not a fish. It is a sea animal. It is not made of jelly. It is made mostly of water.

Some jellyfish are as clear as glass. Others have colors. All are soft and mushy. They come in all sizes.

A jellyfish has many arms. They hang down like soft ribbons. But the soft arms can sting. Stay away!

1. Jellyfish are made mostly of

    ○ A. jelly   ○ B. fish   ○ C. water

2. Why should you stay away from them?

_____

🌀 BrainTeaser 🌀

Read each title. Circle **fiction** or **fact**.

1. How to Build a Go-Cart   **fiction** or **fact**

2. The Singing Noodle   **fiction** or **fact**

3. Dragons at School   **fiction** or **fact**

4. Grow Your Own Corn   **fiction** or **fact**

Morning Jumpstarts: Reading, Grade 1 © 2013 Scholastic Teaching Resources

Name _____   Date _____

FUN Phonics

Write the missing digraph
for each word in the sentence.

Digraphs

ch   sh   th

1. Let's all sit on the cou_____.

2. Paper money is called ca_____.

3. Deb has her first loose too_____.

4. He will wa_____ the dirty pans.

5. Spring starts in the mon_____ of March.

6. We had fruit pun_____ at the party.

Handwriting Helper

✎ Trace. Then write.

question

quick nap

quiet time

Queen May

📖 Ready, Set, READ!

Read. Then answer the questions.

Help!

"Help!" said the fly on the wall.

"Where are you?" asked Tina.

"I am up here," yelled the fly.

Tina looked up to see a talking fly.

"Flies cannot talk!" she said.

"I can," said the fly. "I must!
I am stuck in your room. I cannot get out.
Will you please open the window?"

"Okay," said Tina. "You said, **please**."

1. What was odd about the fly?
   ○ A. It was inside.   ○ B. It could speak.

2. Why did Tina help the fly?

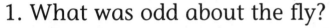

🌀 BrainTeaser 🌀

Write a sentence that uses each word.

1. **elbow** _____

_____

2. **sticky** _____

_____

Morning Jumpstarts: Reading, Grade 1 © 2013 Scholastic Teaching Resources

Name _____ Date _____

FUN Phonics

Fill in the chart. Add **-ing** and **-ed** to each word.
One row is done for you.

Base Word	-ing	-ed
1. show	showing	showed
2. lick		
3. plant		
4. brush		
5. spell		
6. play		

Handwriting Helper

✎ Trace. Then write.

zipper

zigzag

zoom off

zero in

📖 Ready, Set, READ!

Read. Then answer the questions.

Crayon Museum

You can have a great time
at the crayon museum!
You can learn about art.
You can watch crayons get made.
You can see and smell hot wax
in many colors. The wax gets hard
to turn into crayons.
    You can make art there, too.
You can make shadow art with your body
at Cool Moves. You can draw
on the sidewalks at Chalk Walk.

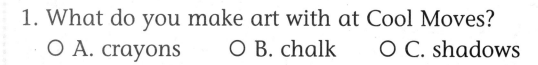

red   green   yellow   blue

1. What do you make art with at Cool Moves?
   ○ A. crayons   ○ B. chalk   ○ C. shadows

2. What are crayons made of? _____

🌀 BrainTeaser 🌀

Write a question that uses each word.

1. **ice** _____

_____

2. **frog** _____

_____

Morning Jumpstarts: Reading, Grade 1 © 2013 Scholastic Teaching Resources

Name _____   Date _____

FUN Phonics

Fill in the chart. Add -**ing** and -**ed** to each word.
One row is done for you.

Base Word	-ing	-ed
1. chew	chewing	chewed
2. mix		
3. reach		
4. part		
5. need		
6. jump		

Handwriting Helper

 Trace. Then write.

joker

join in

jellyroll

juggle

📖 Ready, Set, READ!

Read. Then answer the questions.

Two Dollars

Chet wants a pet. He takes two dollars to the pet shop. "Hi," Chet says. "I have two dollars. What pet can I get?"

The shop man says, "You can get one mouse. Or you can get two fish."

"Two fish, please," says Chet. The man puts two fish in a bag of water. Now Chet has two pets!

1. What did Chet want at first?
   ○ A. money   ○ B. fish   ○ C. a pet

2. Why did the fish go into a bag of water?

_____

🌀 BrainTeaser 🌀

Write a sentence about each picture.

_____

_____

_____

_____

Morning Jumpstarts: Reading, Grade 1 © 2013 Scholastic Teaching Resources

Name _____ Date _____

FUN Phonics

Fill in the chart.
Add **-er** and **-est** to each word.
One row is done for you.

Base Word	-er	-est
1. fast	faster	fastest
2. old		
3. tall		
4. high		
5. young		

Handwriting Helper

✎ Trace. Then write.

ox cart

textbook

Exit sign

six foxes

Morning Jumpstarts: Reading, Grade 1 © 2013 Scholastic Teaching Resources

📖 Ready, Set, READ!

Read. Then answer the questions.

Young Inventor

Abbey Fleck was eight years old. She and her dad were cooking bacon. Then the paper towels ran out. How could they drain off the fat?

Abbey got an idea. A little rack might hold bacon up as it cooked. A tray below would catch the fat.

Abbey tried hard. Soon she made her idea work. She called it the "Makin' Bacon" dish.

1. Which happened first?
   - ○ A. Abbey got an idea.
   - ○ B. Paper towels ran out.
   - ○ C. Abbey and Dad made bacon.

2. How many rows of bacon can the rack hold?

_____

☺ BrainTeaser ☺

Finish each sentence.

1. Kim looked for her lost _____.

2. Zack ran after his _____.

3. Chad hid behind a _____.

4. Ana swam in the _____.

Morning Jumpstarts: Reading, Grade 1 © 2013 Scholastic Teaching Resources

Name _____ Date _____

FUN Phonics

A **compound** word is made up of two short words.
Write the compound word for each picture.

1.   sun + flower = _____

2.   dog + house = _____

3.   flash + light = _____

4.   scare + crow = _____

5.   wheel + chair = _____

Handwriting Helper

✎ Trace. Then write.

on tiptoes

Hurry up!

Hop along

Walk fast

📖 Ready, Set, READ!

Read. Then answer the questions.

Kitten

I wish I had a nickel.
I wish I had a dime.
I wish I had a kitten
to kiss me all the time.

Mom gave me a nickel.
Dad gave me a dime.
Gus gave me a kitten
to kiss me all the time.

I don't miss the nickel.
I don't miss the dime.
Now I have a kitten
to kiss me all the time!

1. Who had a wish?
   ○ A. a kitten   ○ B. a child   ○ C. a parent

2. Who made the wish come true? _____

🌀 BrainTeaser 🌀

Try to spell it!

_____

_____

Morning Jumpstarts: Reading, Grade 1 © 2013 Scholastic Teaching Resources

Name _____   Date _____

FUN Phonics

A **compound** word is made up of two short words. Complete the compound word that names each picture. Use the word bank.

Word Bank

boat	cage
fish	robe
corn	bug

1.	2.	3.
lady_____	bath_____	bird_____
4. 	5.	6.
sail_____	pop_____	star_____

Handwriting Helper

✎ Trace. Then write.

Speak up!

Say cheese!

Sit down.

Morning Jumpstarts: Reading, Grade 1 © 2013 Scholastic Teaching Resources

📖 Ready, Set, READ!

Read. Then answer the questions.

Car Wash Day

Mom parks the car near the hose.
She rolls the windows up tight.
I fill a pail with water and soap.

Next I use the hose to wet the car.
Mom and I rub with big sponges.
Then I spray off the soap.

Last, we wipe away the water
with old rags. We are dirty and wet,
but the car is clean and dry!

1. What are the rags for?
   ○ A. washing   ○ B. drying   ○ C. spraying

2. Why does Mom roll up the windows?

_____

๑ BrainTeaser ๑

Try to spell it!

_____

_____

Morning Jumpstarts: Reading, Grade 1 © 2013 Scholastic Teaching Resources

Name _____   Date _____

FUN Phonics

A **compound** word is made up of two short words. Complete the compound word that names each picture. Use the word bank.

1.	2.	3.
back_____	_____coat	cup_____
4.	5.	6.
_____box	air_____	_____ball

Handwriting Helper

✎ Trace. Then write.

Draw a toy.

Sing a song.

Paint a bird.

📖 Ready, Set, READ!

Read. Then answer the questions.

Worms

Q: What is a worm?

A: A worm is an animal with no legs or bones. It has a mouth but no teeth.

Q: Where do worms live?

A: They live in soil. They dig for food. They cannot live in hot or frozen places.

Q: How do worms move?

A: Worms wiggle bit by bit. Little hairs on their bodies help them inch along.

1. Which does a worm have?
   ○ A. teeth   ○ B. hairs   ○ C. legs

2. Where do worms live?

   _____

🌀 BrainTeaser 🌀

Write **?** for a question. Write **!** to show surprise.

1. Is there room_____

2. Oh, my gosh_____

3. Who is she_____

4. I won the prize_____

Name _____ Date _____

FUN Phonics

Draw lines to match the two words to the **contraction** that means the same. Look for ' where a letter was.

Contract means to <u>get</u> <u>smaller</u>.

I am •	• It's
She is •	• You're
It is •	• She's
We are •	• They're
You are •	• We're
They are •	• I'm

Handwriting Helper

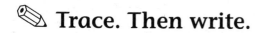

✎ Trace. Then write.

Wiggle out.

Kick a ball.

Dance a jig.

Climb in!

📖 Ready, Set, READ!

Read. Then answer the questions.

Army Ants

Army ants move in big groups.
They march together to find food.
Nothing stops them. Not even big holes.
  Some army ants team up.
They hook legs to make a chain.
More ants hook on. The chain grows.
The ant chain soon reaches across
the hole. It's like a bridge. Other ants
cross it.
  At last the ants unhook and march on.

1. Army ants are special because they move
   ○ A. slowly.   ○ B. in water.   ○ C. in big groups.

2. How do the ants team up?

_____

🌀 BrainTeaser 🌀

Write three words that
start with **sh.**

Write three words that
end with **sh.**

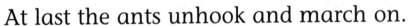

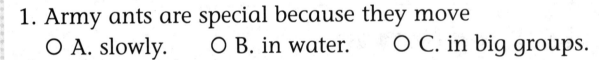

Morning Jumpstarts: Reading, Grade 1 © 2013 Scholastic Teaching Resources

Name _____   Date _____

FUN Phonics

Draw lines to match the two words to the **contraction** that means the same. Look for ' where the letters **wi** were.

Contract means to <u>get</u> <u>smaller</u>.

I will •	• It'll
He will •	• You'll
It will •	• I'll
We will •	• They'll
You will •	• We'll
They will •	• He'll

Handwriting Helper

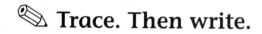

 Trace. Then write.

red cheeks

long legs

two feet

cold toes

Morning Jumpstarts: Reading, Grade 1 © 2013 Scholastic Teaching Resources

📖 Ready, Set, READ!

Read. Then answer the questions.

Cleanup Day

It's cleanup day. Dad turns work into fun. We get rags and mops. We get bottles of cleaner. We are ready!

Dad and I dust and dance. We make faces as we mop. We wiggle when we wipe. We act silly but we work hard.

Soon Dad and I are done. We wash up and change clothes. Then it's time for ice cream!

1. Cleanup Day is fun because Dad gets
   ○ A. busy   ○ B. silly   ○ C. quiet

2. What is the treat when they finish?

_____

🌀 Brain Teaser 🌀

Use all the words to make a sentence.

dry. It hot and is

1. _____

too apple soft. is My

2. _____

Name _____ Date _____

FUN Phonics

Write the **contraction** that fits each sentence.
Use the word bank.

1. It **is not** right to lie. _____

2. They **do not** eat pork. _____

3. We **are not** ready. _____

4. I **cannot** see a thing. _____

5. She **does not** like it. _____

Handwriting Helper

 Trace. Then write.

child's play

check off

chop wood

cheer up

📖 Ready, Set, READ!

Read. Then answer the questions.

Watch Out!

Poison ivy is a plant. It grows in the woods, near roads, and by fields.

Poison ivy leaves have an oil in them. The oil gives people a bad skin rash. The rash itches. It takes days to go away.

Learn how poison ivy looks. If you touch it, you'll be sorry! Remember this:

Leaves of three? Let it be!

1. Poison ivy is

   ○ A. an oil   ○ B. a plant   ○ C. a rash

2. How will you feel if you touch poison ivy?

   _____

☺ Brain Teaser ☺

Circle the word that means the **same**.

shout		silly		quick	
ask	yell	goofy	right	slow	fast

sound		alike		middle	
noise	smell	love	same	end	center

Morning Jumpstarts: Reading, Grade 1 © 2013 Scholastic Teaching Resources

Name _____ Date _____

FUN Phonics

Read each word pair. Circle pairs that **rhyme**.

1. fix	fox		2. plate	wait
3. send	blend		4. knows	road
5. march	porch		6. fry	tie
7. goat	note		8. stick	shock
9. jeep	sleep		10. fudge	bridge

Handwriting Helper

✎ Trace. Then write.

shipshape

short story

shiny shoes

shy sheep

Morning Jumpstarts: Reading, Grade 1 © 2013 Scholastic Teaching Resources

📖 Ready, Set, READ!

Read. Then answer the questions.

Lion and Mouse   A Fable

Lion was asleep. Mouse ran up his tail and woke him. "Stop!" roared Lion. "I will eat you, bad Mouse."

"Sorry!" cried Mouse. "Please free me. I will help you later." Lion **yawned**. He let Mouse go.

That night, Lion fell into a net. He was stuck. Mouse heard Lion roar. He ran to help. Mouse chewed the net to set Lion free.

1. What does the word **yawned** tell about Lion?
   - ○ A. He was hungry.
   - ○ B. He was tired.
   - ○ C. He was yelling.

2. What does the story teach?
   - ○ A. Never wake a lion.
   - ○ B. Stay away from nets.
   - ○ C. Kind acts can be returned.

☺ BrainTeaser ☺

Circle the word that means the **opposite**.

sad		fast		awake	
happy	blue	first	slow	asleep	about

stand		break		push	
reach	sit	fix	brake	drag	pull

Name _____   Date _____

FUN Phonics

Read each word. Write it in the chart where it goes.

| brain | click | flat | grape | mile | pill | shine | track |

Short a	Long a	Short i	Long i

Handwriting Helper

 Trace. Then write.

The Lorax

The Mitten

Owl Moon

Swimmy

📖 Ready, Set, READ!

Read. Then answer the questions.

Happy Clams?

"As happy as a clam" is a saying. But why do people say it? The full saying is "as happy as a clam **at high tide**." So let's think about clams and tides.

At **low tide** the water is not deep. It is when people dig up clams to eat.

At **high tide** the water is deep. It covers the clams. They are safe. No wonder they are happy then!

1. People dig up clams to
   ○ A. help them   ○ B. tickle them   ○ C. eat them

2. Water is deep at _____ tide.

🌀 BrainTeaser 🌀

Fill in a word that makes sense.

1. Penny forgot to _____ her book.

2. The cows go into the _____.

3. Hank hates to eat_____.

4. Will you be my _____?

Name _____ Date _____

FUN Phonics

Read each word. Write it in the chart where it goes.

| blond | dream | edge | flock | roast | seen | test | whole |

Short e	Long e	Short o	Long o

Handwriting Helper

✎ Trace. Then write.

Oh, Susanna

Looby Loo

Shoo Fly

Hokey Pokey

📖 Ready, Set, READ!

Read. Then answer the questions.

Animals of the Desert

The sun **glares**. The desert is dry and very hot.
How do animals stay alive there?

A desert fox has big ears that give off heat.
They help to keep the fox cool. Snakes and lizards
like the heat. They spend the day in the hot sun.

But the sun is too hot for many animals.
They stay underground. At night, they leave
their holes to look for food.

1. The word **glares** means
   ○ A. is cold.   ○ B. shines brightly.   ○ C. goes away.

2. Why do some desert animals hunt at night?

_____

◉ BrainTeaser ◉

Make as many words as you can. Use
ONLY the letters in the wheel. Each word
must have an **E**, plus two or more letters.

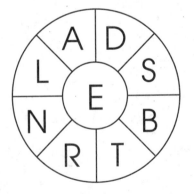

_____

_____

_____

Name _____   Date _____

FUN Phonics

Synonyms mean the same. Match each word on the left with its synonym on the right.

tired •	• pull
pick •	• mend
drag •	• choose
jump •	• tale
fix •	• sleepy
story •	• leap

Handwriting Helper

✎ Trace. Then write.

How are you?

I am fine.

📖 Ready, Set, READ!

Read. Then answer the questions.

Why Bears Have Short Tails

Bear met Fox in the woods one winter day. Fox had many tasty fish.

"How can I get fish?" asked Bear.

Fox said, "Cut a hole in the ice. Hang your long tail down it. Fish will bite your tail. Wait and you will get many fish."

Bear did this. But his long tail got very cold. It broke off when he pulled it up.

And that's why bears have short tails.

1. What kind of story is this?

   ○ A. folktale   ○ B. poem   ○ C. news story

2. How do you know that Bear once had a long tail?

   _____

🌀 BrainTeaser 🌀

Make as many words as you can. Use ONLY the letters in the wheel. Each word must have an **O**, plus two or more letters.

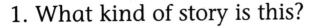

_____

_____

_____

Morning Jumpstarts: Reading, Grade 1 © 2013 Scholastic Teaching Resources

Name _____ Date _____

FUN Phonics

Antonyms are opposites. Match each word on the left with its antonym on the right.

old •	• dry
wet •	• fast
thick •	• new
slow •	• smooth
rich •	• poor
bumpy •	• thin

Handwriting Helper

✎ Trace. Then write.

What is your name?

Where is your lunch?

📖 Ready, Set, READ!

Read.
Then answer the questions.

Polar Bears

Polar bears are white. So is the ice where they live. This makes polar bears hard to see. It helps them hunt. They wait for a seal to get near. They grab it with their long claws.

Polar bears stay warm even in icy water. They have two thick layers of fur. Both layers keep the bear warm. The bear also has thick fat under its fur. This helps too.

1. What is it like where polar bears live?
   - ○ A. icy
   - ○ B. dry
   - ○ C. warm

2. What do polar bears eat?

   _____

   _____

   _____

   _____

⊚ BrainTeaser ⊚

Make as many words as you can. Use ONLY the letters in the wheel. Each word must have an **I**, plus two or more letters.

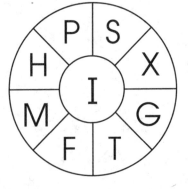

_____

_____

Morning Jumpstarts: Reading, Grade 1 © 2013 Scholastic Teaching Resources

Answers

Jumpstart 1

Fun Phonics: 1. ball 2. key 3. hand 4. pig 5. top 6. web

Handwriting Helper: Check children's work for accuracy and legibility.

Ready, Set, Read!

Go to the park.

Find a book.

Paint a picture.

Ride a bike.

Brainteaser:

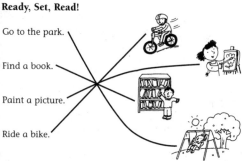

Jumpstart 2

Fun Phonics: 1. cow 2. leg 3. map 4. duck 5. pill 6. fan

Handwriting Helper: Check children's work for accuracy and legibility.

Ready, Set, Read!

Snow falls.

It is raining.

The sun is hot!

It is windy.

Clouds are puffy.

Brainteaser:

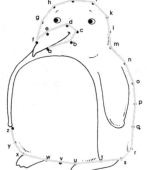

Jumpstart 3

Fun Phonics: 1. salt 2. game 3. nest 4. jeep 5. vine 6. zoo

Handwriting Helper: Check children's work for accuracy and legibility.

Ready, Set, Read! (Top to bottom) humps/camel; tall neck/giraffe; stripes/zebra; mane/lion; trunk/elephant

Brainteaser:

Jumpstart 4

Fun Phonics: 1. crab 2. leaf 3. book 4. broom 5. soap 6. bus

Handwriting Helper: Check children's work for accuracy and legibility.

Ready, Set, Read! (Top to bottom) Tess, Finn, Finn, Tess

Brainteaser:

Jumpstart 5

Fun Phonics: 1. coat 2. jar 3. flag 4. cloud 5. pool 6. moon

Handwriting Helper: Check children's work for accuracy and legibility.

Ready, Set, Read! Hank is the frog in midair; Suzy is swimming in the water.

Brainteaser:

N O P Q R S T	U V W X Y Z
s r p q t n o	x z v u w y

Jumpstart 6

Fun Phonics: 1. pan 2. leg 3. lip 4. fox 5. bud 6. sun

Handwriting Helper: Check children's work for accuracy and legibility.

Ready, Set, Read! 1. A 2. Answers will vary; sample answer: big/strong

Brainteaser:

Big	can	You	not	See	kit
old	Dad	tub	Jet	him	May

Jumpstart 7
Fun Phonics: 1. m 2. g 3. b 4. l 5. v 6. n
Handwriting Helper: Check children's work for accuracy and legibility.
Ready, Set, Read! 1. B 2. The frog will jump.
Brainteaser: Check children's work for accuracy.

Jumpstart 8
Fun Phonics: 1. ham 2. bag 3. cap 4. glass 5. fan 6. pad
Handwriting Helper: Check children's work for accuracy and legibility.
Ready, Set, Read! 1. B 2. No
Brainteaser: Names—Gus, Nan; Places—hill, sea;
Body Words—arm, hip

Jumpstart 9
Fun Phonics: 1. cab 2. crack 3. lamp 4. bend 5. trash 6. bath
Handwriting Helper: Check children's work for accuracy and legibility.
Ready, Set, Read! 1. B 2. two
Brainteaser: Fruits—fig, grapes, plum; Meats—beef, lamb, ham;
Drinks—milk, tea, water

Jumpstart 10
Fun Phonics: 1. crib 2. milk 3. swim 4. dish 5. fist 6. hill
Handwriting Helper: Check children's work for accuracy and legibility.
Ready, Set, Read! 1. B 2. Sample answer: It helps you know what to do and in what order.
Brainteaser: -at words—hat, mat, flat; -ip words—lip, trip, dip

Jumpstart 11
Fun Phonics: 1. lick 2. pin 3. king 4. drip 5. knit 6. clip
Handwriting Helper: Check children's work for accuracy and legibility.
Ready, Set, Read! 1. A 2. Sample answers: You can fly up high; you can look down on things; you feel free.
Brainteaser: -ail words—mail, tail, Gail; -ig words—big, twig, wig

Jumpstart 12
Fun Phonics: 1. box 2. cot 3. mop 4. log 5. sock 6. pond
Handwriting Helper: Check children's work for accuracy and legibility.
Ready, Set, Read! 1. A 2. 1, 3, 5
Brainteaser: -ell words—fell, spell, well; -ot words—dot, spot, not

Jumpstart 13
Fun Phonics: 1. rod 2. stop 3. fox 4. frog 5. knob 6. clock
Handwriting Helper: Check children's work for accuracy and legibility.
Ready, Set, Read! 1. A 2. happy
Brainteaser: -ink words—pink, wink, drink; -ock words—lock, rock, block

Jumpstart 14
Fun Phonics: 1. tub 2. bud 3. mug 4. sun 5. bus 6. hump
Handwriting Helper: Check children's work for accuracy and legibility.
Ready, Set, Read! 1. A 2. strong, solid
Brainteaser: Answers may vary; samples include: -am words—dam, ham, jam, Sam, yam; -op words—bop, cop, hop, mop, pop, stop

Jumpstart 15
Fun Phonics: 1. brush 2. dust 3. plug 4. drum 5. truck 6. skunk
Handwriting Helper: Check children's work for accuracy and legibility.
Ready, Set, Read! 1. B 2. tidy, made, straightened out
Brainteaser: Answers may vary; samples include: -eed words—deed, feed, reed, seed, weed; -est words—chest, jest, nest, rest, test, west

Jumpstart 16
Fun Phonics: 1. hen 2. net 3. tent 4. sled 5. vest 6. step
Handwriting Helper: Check children's work for accuracy and legibility.
Ready, Set, Read! 1. A 2. to keep your brain safe
Brainteaser: 1. bag 2. fin 3. sick

Jumpstart 17
Fun Phonics: 1. belt 2. shell 3. check 4. bench 5. desk 6. bread
Handwriting Helper: Check children's work for accuracy and legibility.
Ready, Set, Read! 1. B 2. A
Brainteaser: Answers will vary; samples include: hop, dog, key, lay, big, dip

Jumpstart 18
Fun Phonics: 1. rake 2. tape 3. vase 4. whale 5. shade 6. skate
Handwriting Helper: Check children's work for accuracy and legibility.
Ready, Set, Read! 1. B 2. A
Brainteaser: Answers will vary; samples include: boil, dish, fact, heel, knob, look

Jumpstart 19
Fun Phonics: 1. sail 2. plate 3. snail 4. tray 5. paint 6. train
Handwriting Helper: Check children's work for accuracy and legibility.
Ready, Set, Read! 1. gardens 2. voles 3. moles
Brainteaser: Answers may vary; most likely choices: 1. o 2. i 3. u

Jumpstart 20
Fun Phonics: 1. nine 2. kite 3. tire 4. pipe 5. hike 6. dime
Handwriting Helper: Check children's work for accuracy and legibility.
Ready, Set, Read! 1. A 2. B 3. Mermaids are not real.
Brainteaser: 1. No dogs. 2. Don't go. 3. Trains cross here.

Jumpstart 21
Fun Phonics: 1. hive 2. slide 3. knife 4. mice 5. smile 6. fly
Handwriting Helper: Check children's work for accuracy and legibility.
Ready, Set, Read! 1. It has no legs. 2. B
Brainteaser: Check children's drawings for accuracy and completeness.

Jumpstart 22
Fun Phonics: 1. cone 2. hole 3. smoke 4. hose 5. crow 6. fold
Handwriting Helper: Check children's work for accuracy and legibility.
Ready, Set, Read! 1. B 2. Four: Bill, Nan, Tom, and Inez
Brainteaser: Check children's drawings for accuracy and completeness.

Jumpstart 23

Fun Phonics: 1. stove **2.** globe **3.** blow **4.** coat **5.** toad **6.** toast
Handwriting Helper: Check children's work for accuracy and legibility.
Ready, Set, Read! 1. B **2.** 53 Gray Lane
Brainteaser:

```
J T C A G E L R
O I U Q U A K O
S R B N E S T S
I E E P M R O E
```

Jumpstart 24

Fun Phonics: 1. mule **2.** fruit **3.** cube **4.** tuba **5.** flute **6.** glue
Handwriting Helper: Check children's work for accuracy and legibility.
Ready, Set, Read! 1. Glen saw his new house. **2.** B
Brainteaser:

```
R O P E K I T H
U P A C A K E O
B U I S W A N W
L A U T K I T E
```

Jumpstart 25

Fun Phonics: 1. new **2.** dune **3.** ruler **4.** suit **5.** screw **6.** juice
Handwriting Helper: Check children's work for accuracy and legibility. Answers will vary.
Ready, Set, Read! 1. B **2.** They are too big; they need deep water.
Brainteaser: (Top to bottom) hug/hugs, ring/rings, look/looks, plate/plates

Jumpstart 26

Fun Phonics: 1. door **2.** sheep **3.** seed **4.** queen **5.** feet **6.** wheel
Handwriting Helper: Check children's work for accuracy and legibility.
Ready, Set, Read! 1. B **2.** A kitten was stuck in the tree. It was crying for help.
Brainteaser: (Top to bottom) room, floor, step

Jumpstart 27

Fun Phonics: 1. tea **2.** seal **3.** bean **4.** leash **5.** beak **6.** beads
Handwriting Helper: Check children's work for accuracy and legibility.
Ready, Set, Read! 1. C **2.** to catch a fish to eat
Brainteaser: 1. peach **2.** fox **3.** kiss **4.** bush

Jumpstart 28

Fun Phonics: (Left to right) frame, draw; price, crack, broom
Handwriting Helper: Check children's work for accuracy and legibility.
Ready, Set, Read! 1. B **2.** Answers will vary; check children's responses.
Brainteaser: 1. sleeps **2.** flies. Answers will vary for 3 and 4; samples include: **3.** crawls, moves **4.** laughs, smiles, grins

Jumpstart 29

Fun Phonics: (Left to right) plane, sleep; blast, globe, flag
Handwriting Helper: Check children's work for accuracy and legibility.
Ready, Set, Read! 1. Sample answer: It tells you that you get some water from what you eat. **2.** A
Brainteaser: (Left to right) jump, rib, shoe; flat, much, when

Jumpstart 30

Fun Phonics: (Left to right) snug, steam or stream, space, smile, scoot
Handwriting Helper: Check children's work for accuracy and legibility.
Ready, Set, Read! 1. C **2.** because she loves food
Brainteaser: (Left to right) line, run, start; boot, horse, ride

Jumpstart 31

Fun Phonics: 1. hand/nd **2.** fact/ct **3.** child/ld **4.** mask/sk **5.** stump/mp **6.** belt/lt
Handwriting Helper: Check children's work for accuracy and legibility.
Ready, Set, Read! 1. A **2.** to get bigger and turn blue
Brainteaser: (Top to bottom) 3-2-1; 3-1-2; 2-3-1; 2-1-3

Jumpstart 32

Fun Phonics: 1. wasp/sp **2.** bird/rd **3.** fork/rk **4.** skunk/nk **5.** fist/st **6.** paint/nt
Handwriting Helper: Check children's work for accuracy and legibility.
Ready, Set, Read! 1. to learn how to swim **2.** B
Brainteaser:

Jumpstart 33

Fun Phonics: 1. thirty **2.** shirt **3.** chicken **4.** shut **5.** chop **6.** think
Handwriting Helper: Check children's work for accuracy and legibility.
Ready, Set, Read! 1. C **2.** Marc Brown and his son
Brainteaser: 1. fox **2.** ant **3.** frog. **4.** hen **5.** duck **6.** pig

Jumpstart 34

Fun Phonics: 1. wheels **2.** phone **3.** When **4.** there **5.** photo **6.** this
Handwriting Helper: Check children's work for accuracy and legibility.
Ready, Set, Read! 1. C **2.** red, white, and blue
Brainteaser: 1. black **2.** brown **3.** green **4.** blue **5.** yellow **6.** pink

Jumpstart 35

Fun Phonics: 1. king **2.** ring **3.** fang **4.** wing **5.** long **6.** sing
Handwriting Helper: Check children's work for accuracy and legibility.
Ready, Set, Read! 1. C **2.** They can sting you.
Brainteaser: 1. fact **2.** fiction **3.** fiction **4.** fact

Jumpstart 36

Fun Phonics: 1. couch **2.** cash **3.** tooth **4.** wash **5.** month **6.** punch
Handwriting Helper: Check children's work for accuracy and legibility.
Ready, Set, Read! 1. B **2.** The fly said please.
Brainteaser: Answers will vary; check children's sentences.

Jumpstart 37

Fun Phonics: 2. licking, licked **3.** planting, planted
4. brushing, brushed **5.** spelling, spelled **6.** playing, played
Handwriting Helper: Check children's work for accuracy and legibility.
Ready, Set, Read! 1. C **2.** wax
Brainteaser: Questions will vary; check children's work.

Jumpstart 38

Fun Phonics: 2. mixing, mixed **3.** reaching, reached
4. parting, parted **5.** needing, needed **6.** jumping, jumped
Handwriting Helper: Check children's work for accuracy and legibility.
Ready, Set, Read! 1. C **2.** So Chet could take them home
Brainteaser: Sentences will vary; check children's work.

Jumpstart 39

Fun Phonics: 2. older, oldest **3.** taller, tallest **4.** higher, highest
5. younger, youngest
Handwriting Helper: Check children's work for accuracy and legibility.
Ready, Set, Read! 1. C **2.** three
Brainteaser: Answers will vary; check that children's sentences make sense.

Jumpstart 40

Fun Phonics: 1. sunflower **2.** doghouse **3.** flashlight
4. scarecrow **5.** wheelchair
Handwriting Helper: Check children's work for accuracy and legibility.
Ready, Set, Read! 1. B **2.** Gus
Brainteaser: (Left to right) butterfly, snowflake

Jumpstart 41

Fun Phonics: 1. ladybug **2.** bathrobe **3.** birdcage **4.** sailboat
5. popcorn **6.** starfish
Handwriting Helper: Check children's work for accuracy and legibility.
Ready, Set, Read! 1. B **2.** to keep water out of the inside of the car
Brainteaser: (Left to right) mailbox, grasshopper

Jumpstart 42

Fun Phonics: 1. backpack **2.** raincoat **3.** cupcake **4.** lunchbox
5. airplane. **6.** football
Handwriting Helper: Check children's work for accuracy and legibility.
Ready, Set, Read! 1. B **2.** Worms live in soil.
Brainteaser: 1. ? **2.** ! **3.** ? **4.** !

Jumpstart 43

Fun Phonics: (Top to bottom) She is/She's; It is/It's; We are/We're; You are/You're; They are/They're
Handwriting Helper: Check children's work for accuracy and legibility.
Ready, Set, Read! 1. C **2.** They hook their legs together.
Brainteaser: Answers will vary; check that children's words fit the rules.

Jumpstart 44

Fun Phonics: (Top to bottom) He will/He'll; It will/It'll; We will/We'll; You will/you'll; They will/They'll
Handwriting Helper: Check children's work for accuracy and legibility.
Ready, Set, Read! 1. B **2.** ice cream
Brainteaser: 1. It is hot and dry. **2.** My apple is too soft.

Jumpstart 45

Fun Phonics: 1. isn't **2.** don't **3.** aren't **4.** can't **5.** doesn't
Handwriting Helper: Check children's work for accuracy and legibility.
Ready, Set, Read! 1. B **2.** itchy
Brainteaser: (Left to right) yell, goofy, fast; noise, same, center

Jumpstart 46

Fun Phonics: Pairs 2, 3, 6, 7, and 9 rhyme.
Handwriting Helper: Check children's work for accuracy and legibility.
Ready, Set, Read! 1. B **2.** C
Brainteaser: (Left to right) happy, slow, asleep; sit, fix, pull

Jumpstart 47

Fun Phonics: short *a*—flat, track; long *a*—brain, grape; short *i*—click, pill; long *i*—mile, shine
Handwriting Helper: Check children's work for accuracy and legibility.
Ready, Set, Read! 1. C **2.** high
Brainteaser: Answers will vary; check children's sentences.

Jumpstart 48

Fun Phonics: short *e*—edge, test; long *e*—dream, seen; short *o*—blond, flock; long *o*—roast, whole
Handwriting Helper: Check children's work for accuracy and legibility.
Ready, Set, Read! 1. B **2.** It's too hot during the day.
Brainteaser: Answers will vary; check that children's words include *e* and two more letters, and are spelled correctly.

Jumpstart 49

Fun Phonics: (Top to bottom) pick/choose; drag/pull; jump/leap; fix/mend; story/tale
Handwriting Helper: Check children's work for accuracy and legibility.
Ready, Set, Read! 1. A **2.** The story tells us, and the long tail broke off.
Brainteaser: Answers will vary; check that children's words include *o* and two more letters, and are spelled correctly.

Jumpstart 50

Fun Phonics: (Top to bottom) wet/dry; thick/thin; slow/fast; rich/poor; bumpy/smooth
Handwriting Helper: Check children's work for accuracy and legibility.
Ready, Set, Read! 1. A **2.** seals
Brainteaser: Answers will vary; check that children's words include *i* and two more letters, and are spelled correctly.